teacher's friend publications

Preschool Basic Skills

Visual Perception and Drawing Activities

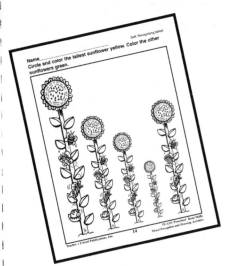

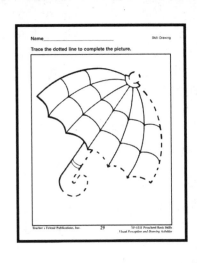

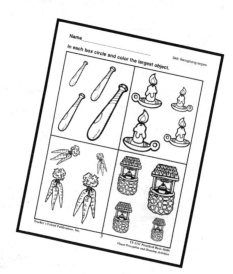

Basic visual perception and drawing activities necessary for developing the skills students need to succeed!

Written by: Aaron Levy & Kelley Wingate Levy
Illustrated by: Karen Sevaly

Look for all of Teacher's Friend's Basic Skills Books at your local educational retailer!

Table of Contents

teacher's friend publications

ISBN-13 978-0-439-50026-5
ISBN-10 0-439-50026-5

In each box circle and color the largest object.

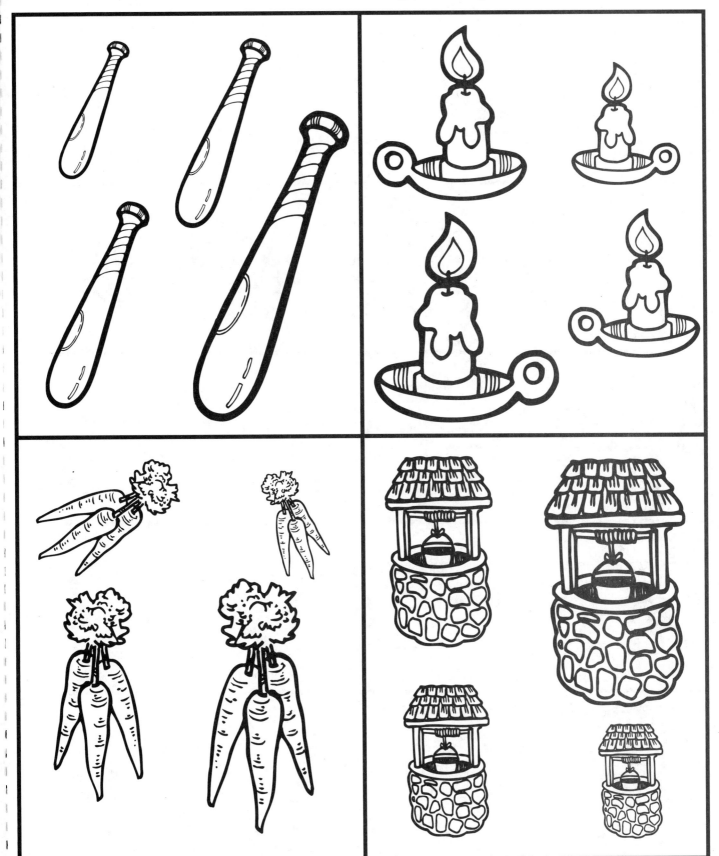

Circle and color the largest object in each row.

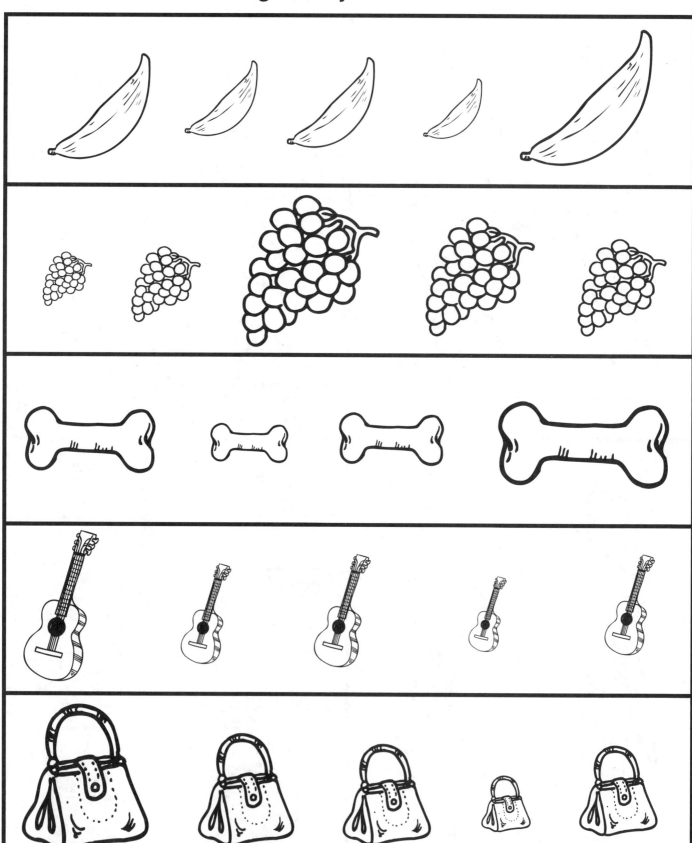

Name_____

Circle and color the largest object in each row.

TF-1311 Preschool Basic Skills
Visual Perception and Drawing Activities

Name_____

In each box circle and color the smallest object.

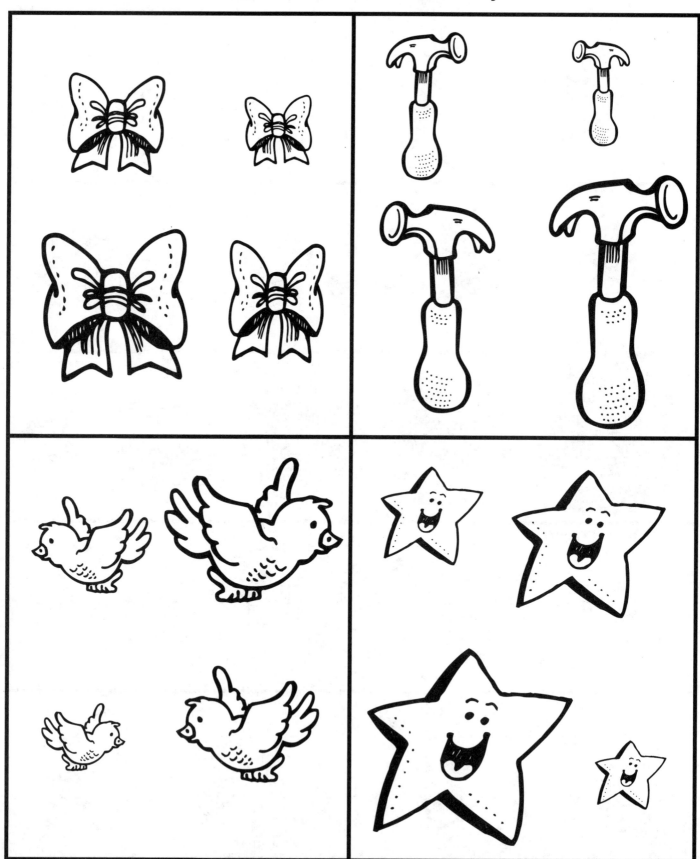

TF-1311 Preschool Basic Skills
Visual Perception and Drawing Activities

Name_____

Circle and color the smallest object in each row.

Circle and color the smallest object in each row.

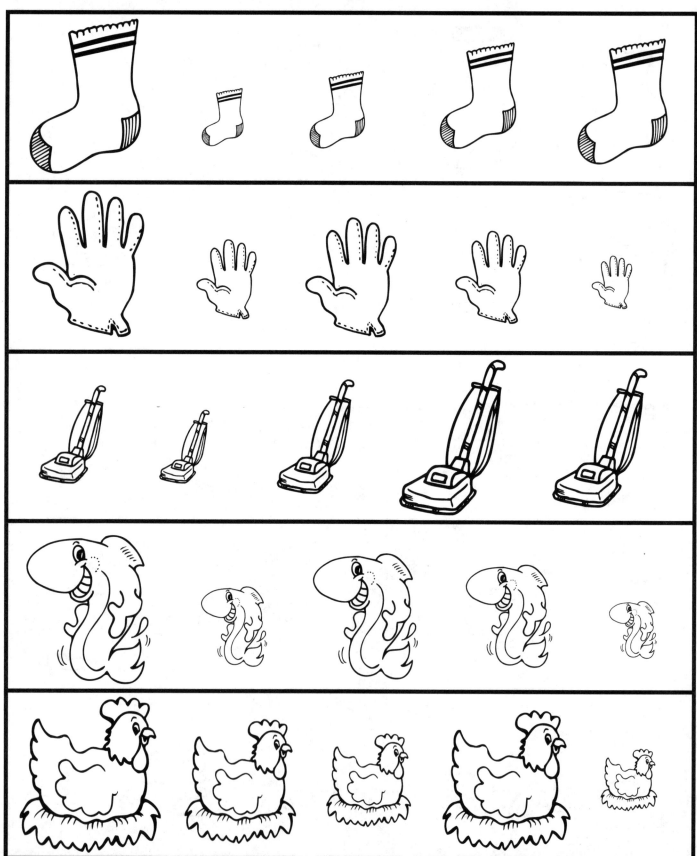

Name_____

Color all of the large apples red.
Color all of the small apples green.

Color all of the large cakes yellow.
Color all of the small cakes brown.

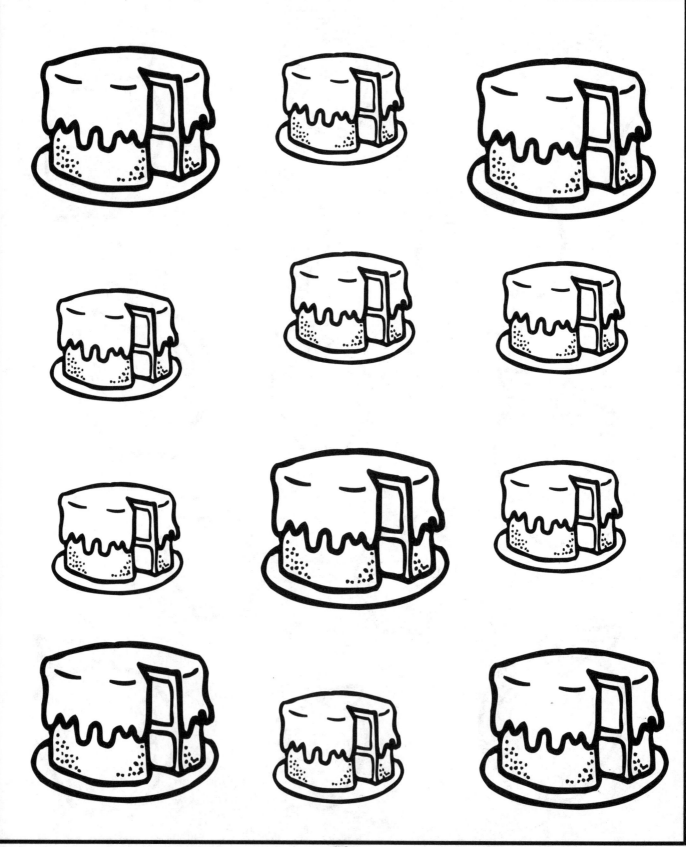

Name_____

Color all of the large ice cream cones red.
Color all of the small ice cream cones blue.

Visual Perception and Drawing Activities

Name_____

Circle and color the longest object in each box.

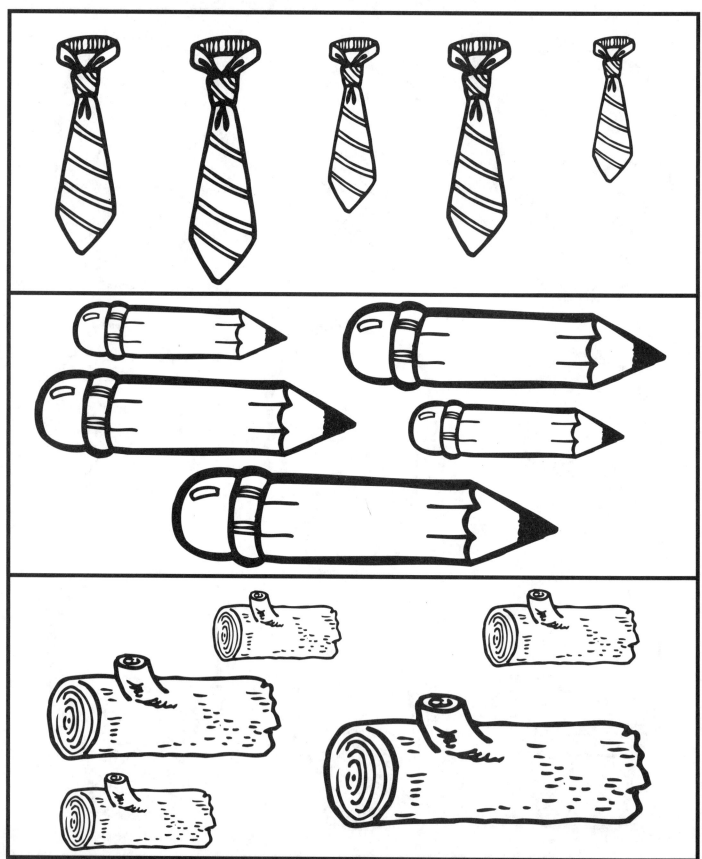

12
TF-1311 Preschool Basic Skills
Visual Perception and Drawing Activities

Name_____

Color the long toothbrushes blue.
Color the short toothbrushes green.

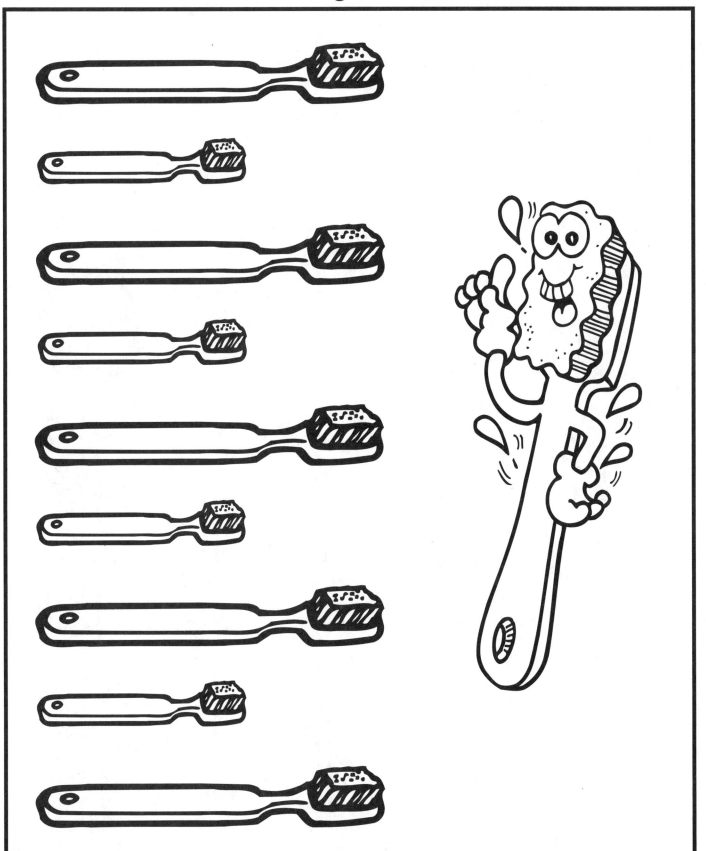

Circle and color the tallest sunflower yellow.
Color the other sunflowers green.

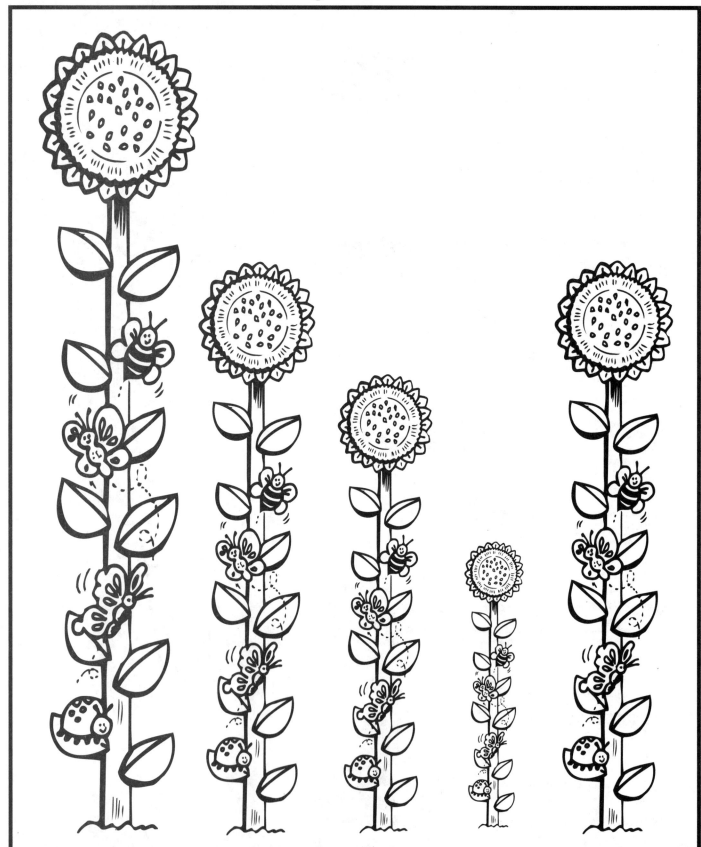

Name_____

Circle and color the objects that are the same in each box.

Circle and color the objects that are the same in each box.

Name_____

In each row color the objects that are the same as the first one.

Name_____

In each row color the objects that are the same as the first one.

Draw a line to match the objects that are the same.

Name_____

Draw a line to match the objects that are the same.

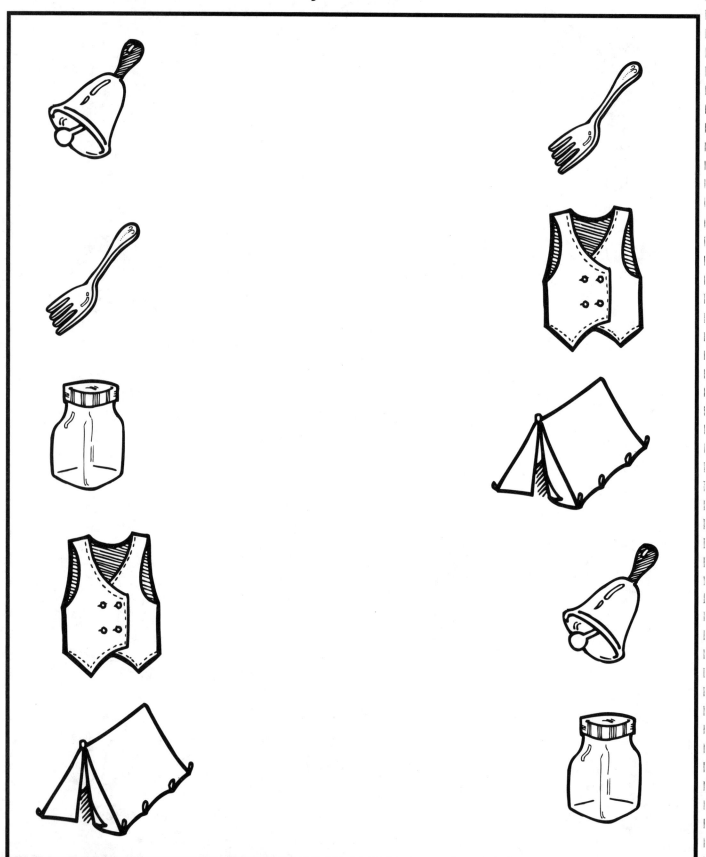

Draw a line to match the objects that are the same.

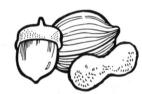

Circle and color the object that is different in each box.

Circle and color the object that is different in each box.

Name_____

Circle and color the object that is different in each row.

TF-1311 Preschool Basic Skills
Visual Perception and Drawing Activities

Name_____

Skill: Recognizing alike and different

Color the object that is different in each row.

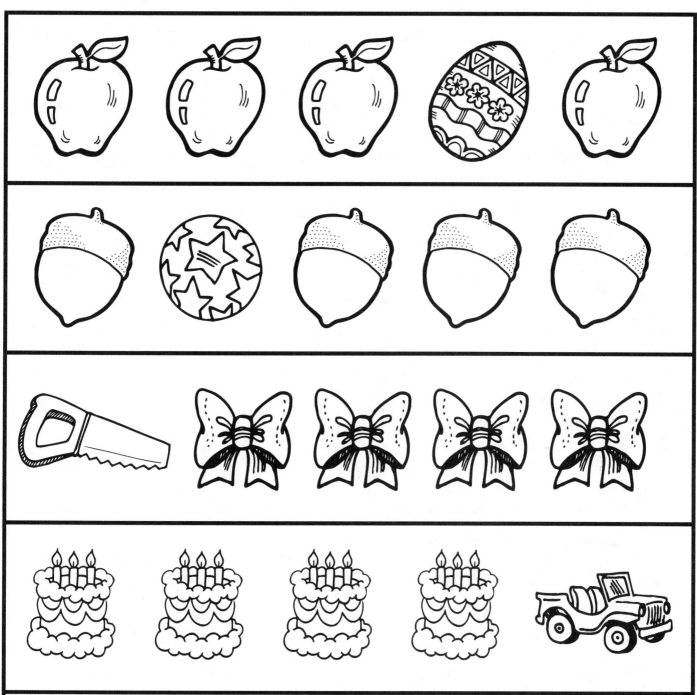

Visual Perception and Drawing Activities

Name_____

Color the shape that is different in each row.

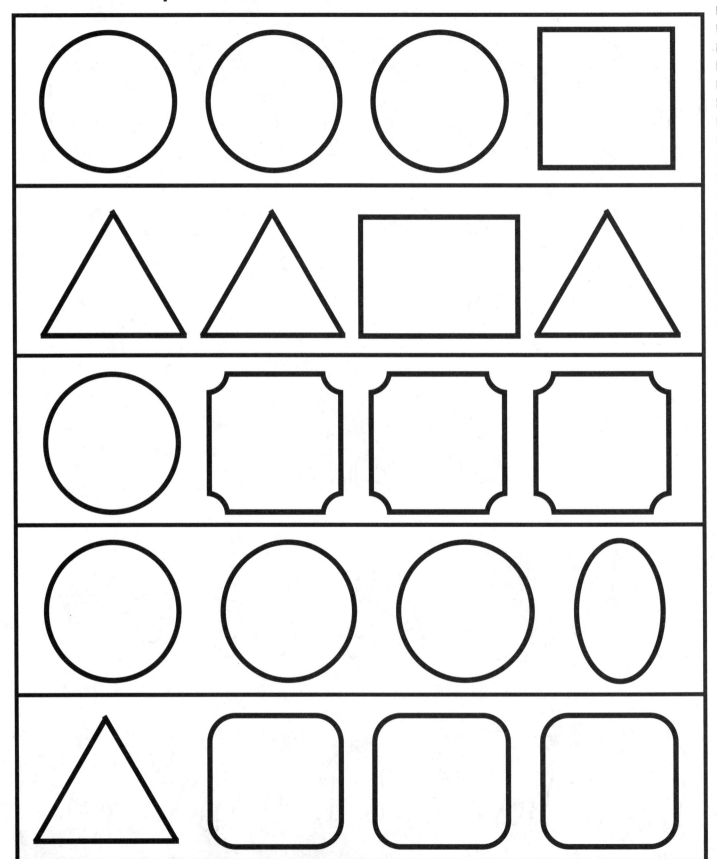

26
TF-1311 Preschool Basic Skills
Visual Perception and Drawing Activities

Trace the dotted line to complete the picture.

TF-1311 Preschool Basic Skills
Visual Perception and Drawing Activities

Trace the dotted line to complete the picture.

TF-1311 Preschool Basic Skills
Visual Perception and Drawing Activities

Trace the dotted line to complete the picture.

Name_____

Trace the dotted line to complete the picture.

Trace the dotted lines to complete the pizza. Add your favorite toppings and color the pizza.

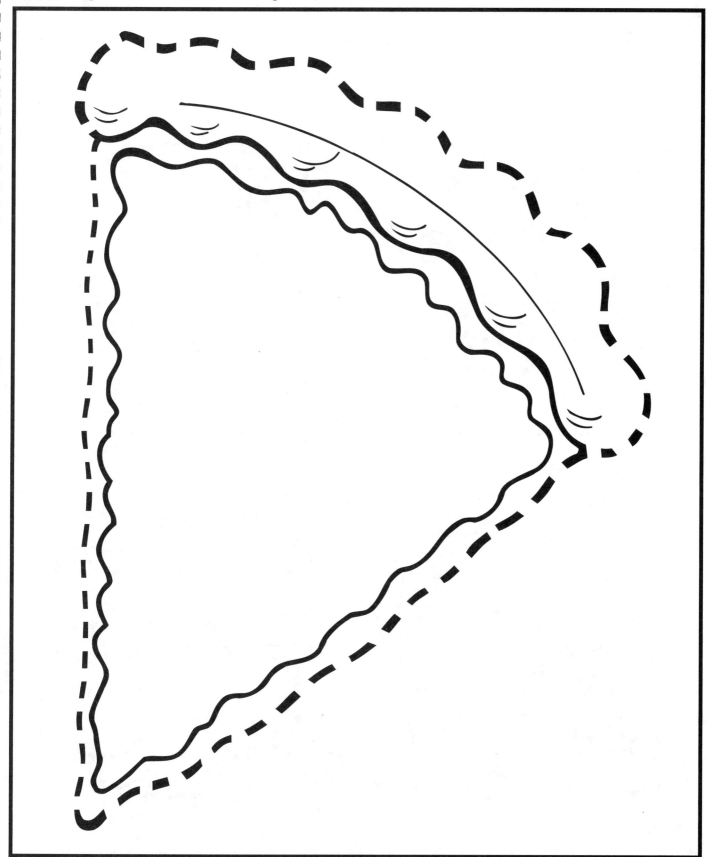

Name_____

In each box make the second picture look like the first one.

Name_____

In each box make the second picture look like the first one.

　　33　　**TF-1311 Preschool Basic Skills**
Visual Perception and Drawing Activities

In each box make the second picture look like the first one.

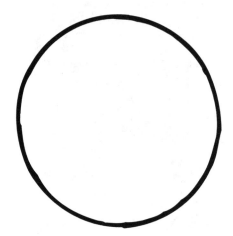

Follow the steps to draw your own bee.

Name_____

Follow the steps to draw your own bear.

1.

2.

3.

Name_____

Follow the steps to draw your own cat.

Follow the steps to draw your own flower.

Follow the steps to draw your own turkey.

Follow the steps to draw your own frog.

1.

2.

3.

Draw a picture of what you might see through a telescope.

Draw a picture of what you might see underwater.

Skill: Drawing

Draw a picture of what you might see from the sky.

43 **TF-1311 Preschool Basic Skills**
Visual Perception and Drawing Activities

Draw a picture of your family in the picture frame.

Draw a picture of yourself.

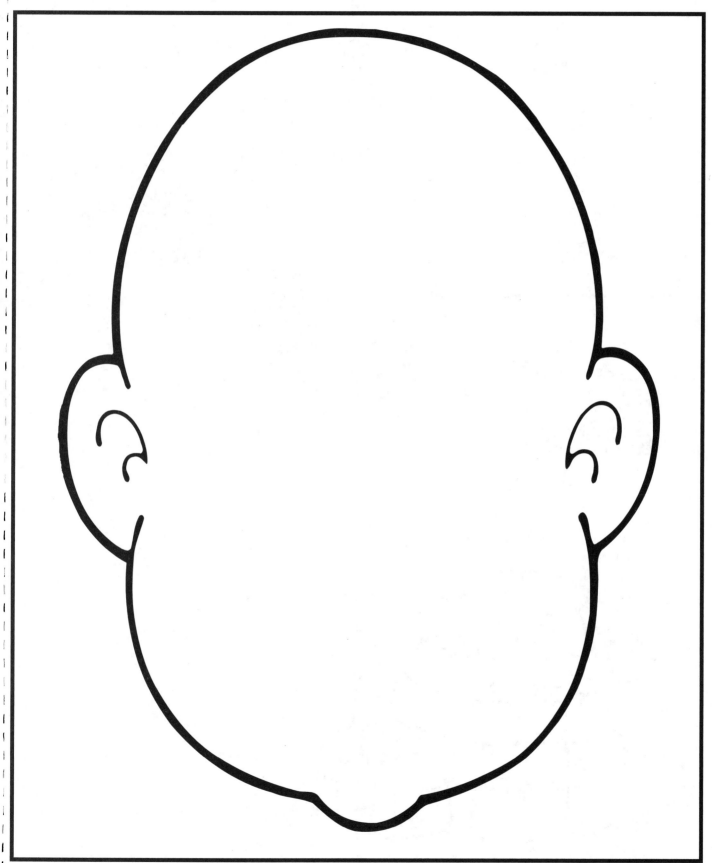

TF-1311 Preschool Basic Skills
Visual Perception and Drawing Activities

Name_____

Draw an Eskimo, like the one below, next to the igloo.

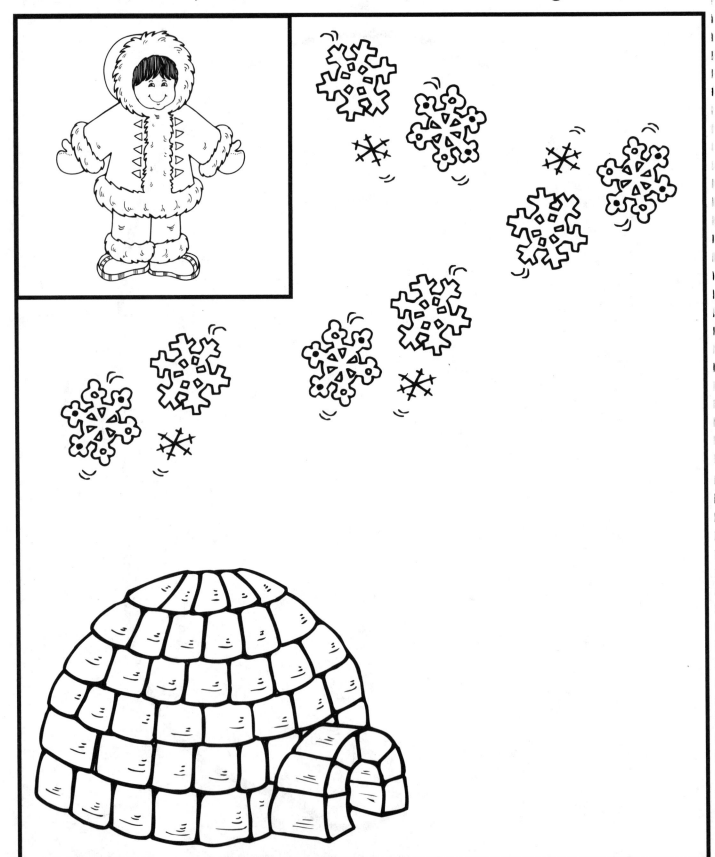

TF-1311 Preschool Basic Skills
Visual Perception and Drawing Activities

Draw a giraffe, like the one below, next to the tree.

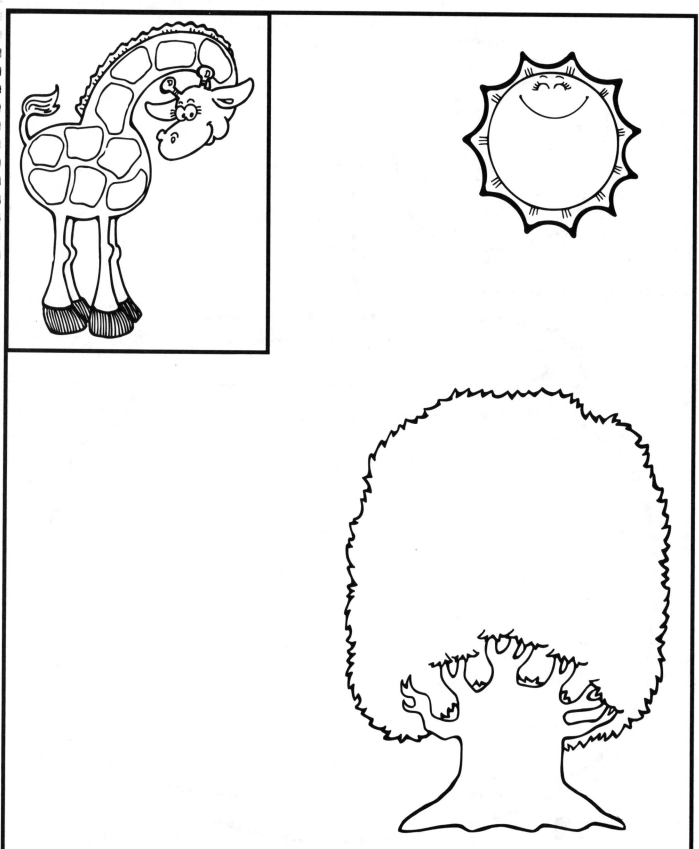

Draw a fish, like the one below, in the fish bowl.